Please Read With Your Bible

11/20/22

A HANDBOOK *for* NEW BELIEVERS

SHELLEANN M. BROWN

WESTBOW
PRESS®
A DIVISION OF THOMAS NELSON
& ZONDERVAN

Copyright © 2022 Shelleann M. Brown.

All rights reserved. No part of this book may be used or reproduced by any means, graphic, electronic, or mechanical, including photocopying, recording, taping or by any information storage retrieval system without the written permission of the author except in the case of brief quotations embodied in critical articles and reviews.

This book is a work of non-fiction. Unless otherwise noted, the author and the publisher make no explicit guarantees as to the accuracy of the information contained in this book and in some cases, names of people and places have been altered to protect their privacy.

WestBow Press books may be ordered through booksellers or by contacting:

WestBow Press
A Division of Thomas Nelson & Zondervan
1663 Liberty Drive
Bloomington, IN 47403
www.westbowpress.com
844-714-3454

Because of the dynamic nature of the Internet, any web addresses or links contained in this book may have changed since publication and may no longer be valid. The views expressed in this work are solely those of the author and do not necessarily reflect the views of the publisher, and the publisher hereby disclaims any responsibility for them.

Any people depicted in stock imagery provided by Getty Images are models, and such images are being used for illustrative purposes only. Certain stock imagery © Getty Images.

Scripture marked (KJV) taken from the King James Version of the Bible.

Scripture quotations marked (AMP) are taken from the Amplified Bible, Copyright © 1954, 1958, 1962, 1964, 1965, 1987 by The Lockman Foundation. Used by permission.

ISBN: 978-1-6642-6545-5 (sc)
ISBN: 978-1-6642-6547-9 (hc)
ISBN: 978-1-6642-6546-2 (e)

Library of Congress Control Number: 2022908073

Print information available on the last page.

WestBow Press rev. date: 07/29/2022

Contents

Introduction vii

Chapter 1   Lifestyle Changes 1
Chapter 2   Prayer 9
Chapter 3   Fasting 29
Chapter 4   Reading and Understanding the Word 39
Chapter 5   Tithes and Offerings 45
Chapter 6   Testimony 51
Chapter 7   Sanctification 61
Chapter 8   The Holy Spirit 67
Chapter 9   Communion 75
Chapter 10 Doctrine and Church Culture 81
Chapter 11 Discipleship 87

AMEN 93
Acknowledgments 95
References 97

Introduction

Just as it is for a newborn babe, so should it be for a new believer in Christ. The process of nurturing ought to be done with patience, care, and godly love. A new believer is an individual who has recently declared Jesus Christ as Lord and Savior of their life and is about ready to give up their previous walk to follow where He leads (Matthew 4:19). This newness brings about a change of heart, mind, soul, body, and spirit.

Evangelism is not new to the body of Christ. As a matter of fact, it is an example set by Christ Himself and a commission left for us to follow in the church of the living God today (Matthew 28:18–20). Spreading the gospel throughout the world and inviting others to accept Jesus as Lord and Savior is our sole responsibility as disciples of Christ. After we have worked tirelessly to organize evangelistic services, we anticipate new souls to be won for the body of Christ. The same labor is needed to move them forward spiritually after they have accepted the call. Thus, the need for a simple handbook to help them along the way. Too often I encounter persons that have accepted Christ as Lord and Savior who are basically 'left on their own to fend for themselves'. They wonder around with questions such as:

1. ***What do I do now?***
   If this is a concern of yours as a new believer, seek help from one who is having a consistent relationship with Christ. I promise you; the Holy Spirit will lead you to the right person (s).
2. ***Who do I speak with about this new decision?***
   Write your many questions, seek a meeting with your Pastor/Spirit Leader and share your concerns. They should put the necessary programs and individuals in place to meet your early needs (Acts 6:1-7)
3. ***Where do I go for help?***
   Go to a church whose core example is the Bible. The help that you desire at this time will be found in the Word of God. The challenges that you are faced with were also encountered by others in the church before you, trust me; they know 'baby talk' and can help.
4. ***Why do I feel so helpless?***
   Feeling helpless at this point in your new walk is normal; hence, "*Casting all your cares upon Him for He careth for you.*" 1 Peter 5:7 KJV. He is a great listener to every conversation; so, go ahead and talk with Him (Psalm 19: 3).
5. ***When will someone explain to me, 'what to do differently?'***
   Take it slow, not to the point of declining, but to the position of being kind to yourself and remembering that you're a baby in Christ. You are still at creeping

stage and is not expected to be walking. Remember the process is timely but should progress forward, because God is a sustaining and maintaining Father of all fathers (Psalm 32:8). He is patient with you, so be timely with yourself.

6. *How do I 'turn things around?'*
   Only God can turn things around in your life (Matthew 6:27). You will start noticing the changes after your past life start looking like something you would never go back to. Turning things around is simply turning your back on your past and start looking toward the future in Christ.

After looking at the previous questions, it is only critical that this book be written for the body of Christ at large, and not for a particular church. The manuscript is set up in a way that all new believers can personally interact with its material, regardless of their denomination.

There will be questions at intervals that readers need to stop and answer. Some instructions will prompt readers to take physical actions, while there are some incomplete scripture verses that will cause you to turn the pages of your Bible. There are several scripture references during your interaction with this book. Therefore, I recommend that you keep an open Bible alongside you while delving your copy. You should keep abreast of what scripture says about your new walk with God. A notebook, pen, and/or pencil, at least two different-colored highlighters, and book markers will do you a world of good. You will be able to make notes and mark important passages in both your Bible and handbook alike. Give yourself simple assignments that will expand your understanding. Homeschool is a taboo for some, but with a pandemic of this nature (Corona Virus/Covid 2019) it would be wise for a new believer to take the opportunity to understand God more at your own pace from home. A hidden curriculum is a lesson learnt without been taught. In other words, take the time out with God to develop some new values, norms and morals that will change some of your old doings and be transformed to the newness of life in this your new walk (Ephesians 4:20-32).

At no time should this handbook replace your Bible.

Chapter 1
LIFESTYLE CHANGES

Welcome to the body of Christ. This is the best independent decision that you will ever make in your life. The Holy Spirit has knocked on your heart's door. You opened and let Him in. Then you made a public declaration to serve Him in believer's baptism.

Now that you are joint heir with Christ according to Romans 8:17, acknowledge how important you are to the body of Christ as you meditate on 1 Corinthians 12:12–27. Jesus has stated, "No longer do I call you servants … but friends" (John 15:15 NKJV).

A new believer suggest that one has been converted from an old lifestyle to a new in Christ (Acts 9:3–6 and Colossians 2:12). Your new walk entails a willingness to adjust to some form of change as it relates to being a new creature (2 Corinthians 5:17 and Ephesians 4:22–32). Even your very line of convocation should begin to change. It is often said that 'no word is bad.' This grants the right to speak words that bring no glory to God but rather gratifying the flesh, such as cursing, lying, blaspheming, and swearing. It is imperative that a new believer start speaking life since they are coming out of a world of sin and death (Proverbs 18:21 and 2 Timothy 2:16–17).

Like a newborn who hungers for milk to develop, the new believer longs for the things of God to grow spiritually (1 Peter 2:1–2). If the associates you had before coming to Christ are not able to help you spiritually, then gradually leave their company and seek others who are able to lift you up (Romans 16:17 and Matthew 15:14). After you are strengthened, go back for your families and friends, then bring them into the fold with you. You have put off the old self and its practices and put on the garments of righteousness (Colossians 3:9–10).

Lifestyle changes may include changing songs you used to listen to, places you used to go, and time you used to give to gossip. You should now be occupied with prayer, reading your Bible, seeking the face of God, and listing to what the Holy Spirit have to say about your new relationship. This developing spiritual bond between you and the Lord will not affect your natural life's settings negatively in no way. It will only add a positive overflow of blessings unto the remainder of your life and those around you.

You may have friends, coworkers, and family members who have been saved for a long time and never saw fit to introduce Christ to you. However, once you surrendered to the call of God, they are prepared to criticize what you do and how you do it. They may tell you that you are going the wrong way, you are not yet saved, or you are in the wrong church. Romans 14 speaks to who they are.

There are also unhealthy Christians in church; beware of them (Philippians 3:2). They make it their duty to cloud your mind with wrongdoing that may have taken place years ago in the church, which will spoil you (Colossians 2:8). This kind of behavior will eat away at your baby-stage salvation and wither you before you get a chance to experience the fullness of what God has in store for you.

Jesus brings to light how cunning the enemy is and how he will deceive you at any cost (Matthew 13:4 and Mark 4:4). You are warned to be careful about which ground you fall on after you have come to know the truth of God through salvation.

Regarding lifestyle changes, you could look at the topic of tattoos. If you were saved after getting a tattoo, leave it alone; it is there as a swift reminder of where you came from and where you will never return. However, if you did not have a tattoo before you were saved, think before you seek one afterward. Ask yourself the following questions and answer them with all sincerity.

- Is it necessary? _____
- Will it bring glory to God? _____
- Will it allow you to grow spiritually in your new faith?
  _____

Read Leviticus 19:28, 2 Corinthians 5:17, and Hebrews 10:26 aloud.

As a new babe in Christ, in order to maintain the peace of Jesus and live an exemplary life, at times you may need to apologize or pay a debt that is owed. This does not mean you are weak or have become 'soft'. You are now making a public declaration that you are a different person in character and is willing to do what is right in the sight of God. Keep in mind that righteousness is simply doing what is right. You will be respected for it.

If you are finding it challenging to do what is right, ask a righteous, praying person in the church to pray you through your struggles. Remember, as a new believer, you need to ask the Holy Spirit to help you in making the right decisions and helping you to choose the best midwives in your circle at this point of your journey. Thus, do not just go to anyone with your life's experiences, but rather choose someone who is holy before the Lord. Be patient when making these decisions, they can make and/or break you; be careful.

Now stop! Reflect on whom you may have wronged, intentionally or unintentionally (Matthew 5:23– 24). Seek to deal with the situation as soon and peaceably as possible. It might even come down to you giving up your right for peace's sake. Giving up your right is allowing the other individual to have the upper hand and the last say. We sometimes take the lower seat for peace's sake; let it go. That might be the necessary thing to do in that situation. If the other party still holds that you were wrong in the matter, let it go. Apologize and move on. It might save your life and someone else's. Do not get wary or give up at this point, continue to do the right thing though it may seem difficult.

Pastor Charles F. Stanley wrote on pg. 16 of his book entitled How to let God Solve Your Problems. *"If you give up now, there is no telling what you will miss."* Do not set up yourself to miss out on anything that God have to offer you; by letting go too soon. Yes! Too soon can be a hundred years from to date. Continue to live in the hope that all your wrongs can be made right through Christ.

Being a child of God does not come down to who is right or wrong, weak or strong. It comes down to who is able to settle conflict and maintain peace (Romans 14:19) in a timely manner. Now that you choose to put God at the head of your life, let Him fight your battles (Deuteronomy 3:2). You will win some of your most difficult battles with a silent tongue (James 1: 19).

If there are matters that need resolving and are worthy

of being fixed, the Holy Spirit will bring those situations to your memory. As you are reminded of varying occurrences, get the help needed to deal with them. Do not put them off. You may get only one chance of resolving the problem. The Holy Spirit will help you if you yield to His leading (John 14:26). If the person is deceased or lives in another country, and you no longer have contact with them, then there is little or nothing that you can do. Ask an elder to pray with you and be willing to accept God's gracious forgiveness and move on (Mark 3:28).

If you are willing to make the necessary changes in your new walk, work at them. This will benefit your spiritual growth greatly.

Notes

Chapter 2
PRAYER

Talking with or to God may not change your language, accent, posture, and so forth; unless you are led by the Holy Spirit to do so. Prayer is very important throughout your walk with God, and even more so as a new believer. Neonatal death can take place if you lack prayer at this early stage (Mark 14:38).

Jesus told Peter to "watch and pray," (Matthew 26:41KJV), while Paul implores us to "pray without ceasing" (1 Thessalonians 5:17 KJV). Prayer is really talking with God on a one-on-one level, which is expected in all healthy relationships. So, keep the communication flowing; He wants to hear from you daily.

Prayers do not need to be long nor loud in order to be effective or heard by your heavenly Father (Matthew 6:5–6). On the other hand, do not misunderstand Matthew 6:5–6 by thinking that God does not require us to stand in the streets and pray—in fact, if that is what the Holy Spirit wants you to do; go ahead. In reference to persons who perform for an applause from a body of people, is a different forum of discussion. He suggests that we come to Him personally, in secret, and then influence others outwardly.

It is recorded in the gospels that Jesus prayed several different prayers throughout His mission here on earth. That example, we should follow. Some of His prayers were long; in fact, Jesus fasted and prayed for forty days and nights in the wilderness (Matthew 4:2). Others were agonizing, as in the garden of Gethsemane (Matthew 26:36–46, Mark 14:32–42 and Luke 22:39–46). He prayed nationally and intentionally for present and future disciples in John 17th chapter. He also had many precise prayers of ordered authority (Matthew 27:46, Luke 23:34, 46 and John 11:43).

The Lord's Prayer or a Format?

In local, national, and international churches, schools, and homes, in both written and spoken contexts, people use the term *'the Lord's Prayer'* out of context. This prayer arrangement is mentioned in two of the synoptic gospels, namely Matthew 6 and Luke 11.

In fact, the Lord's prayers (implying that Jesus prayed) are found throughout all four gospels of the New Testament, especially in John 17; where Jesus prayed for his present and future disciples before going to the cross.

Matthew 6:9–13 is a format that Jesus uses to teach us how to pray. A format gives a clear outline of how to organize something in order to get it right. As mentioned in Matthew 6:9–13, our prayers should begin with acknowledging God and end with glorifying Him.

***

Attempt these seven steps separately until you understand them. Then complete them together. A diversity of Bible version can be used when looking at Matthew 6:9-13. It is recommended that you gather your information from different sources as it will widen your scope of study and have a better appreciation of other people's view point.

1. "Our Father which art in heaven." Acknowledge with whom you are about to have dialogue. Among the gods of this world, you need to make it quite clear to whom you pray. *"Call Him by His name,"* Lucy A. Bennett wrote.

*Call Him by His Name of Jesus, Sweetest name
in heav'n or earth
His name of Jesus in heav'n or earth
Blessed hallowed name of Jesus, Who can fully
speak its worth.
Oh precious name! matchless worth.*

Differentiate the Lord Jesus Christ by character and sovereignty as there are many gods in the earth today. To address an individual in a room full with people you need to call him/her by their name. There are many names of God, a few of those names are mentioned in chapter 6, capitalize on them as you seek to know others during your personal encounter with the Lord.

To whom do you pray? _____

2. "Hallowed be Thy Name." Exalt Him above all else. After you have declared to whom you are talking, you should worship Him. Worshipping God early in your prayer will denounce, banish, and disqualify all other forces that might be lingering as you enter into reasoning with God. Personally proclaim who He is in your life. Reflect for a while. Make a list of the words, attributes, and names that you use to honor the Father of all fathers:

_____
_____
_____
_____

3. "Thy kingdom come, Thy will be done in earth as it is in heaven." Proclaim His authority here, there, and everywhere. Do not confuse 'God's will be done' with 'God been in charge'; there is a big difference. Though He has ultimate knowledge of all things, His will is not always done in our lives, due to free choice we do the things that satisfies us, which in some cases are not God's will on earth. Knowing and doing God's will takes some discipline and obedience on our part. Understand that His will is clearly outlined in the Bible, but the timing is up to us. Are you willing to do His will now? Some persons have been promising God for years that they will serve Him—later.

    Pause and thank God that you are here today. Say, "Lord, take me as I am, [your name]." As you pray, surrender your all to Him and ask that His will be done in your life right now. Do not be afraid to ask Him what His will for your life is. You might be surprised at the simple answer.

4. "Give us this day our daily bread." Ask for your needs to be supplied. Note: request your needs, not your wants. Do not ask amiss (James 4:3). It is not that God is unable to supply both, but He would rather do so when you are able to manage it. He is a loving God and would not want you to leave Him and/or lose your way because you are so overwhelmed with earthly things that you no longer have time to give Him thanks. He might be awaiting your maturity before making you a steward over much (Matthew 25:21). Take a break and identify your top needs

and a few wants. Watch over time as you pray, if you need to alter your items in any way, shape, or form. Remember that your needs are more than food, clothes, and shelter. They also include health, salvation for family, worldwide peace, coverage for the innocent; just to name a few. Your needs are based on your heart's desires in life.

Needs Date:	**Wants** Date:

5. "And forgive us our debts, as we forgive our debtors." Plead for forgiveness to be extent to you as you forgive others. The word *'as'* in the above quotation is not a coincidence. It is a carefully selected word used by Christ to compare the extent or degree to which a thing is measured. Before you ask God to forgive your sin(s), measure to what degree you forgive others. Because the same quantity and quality of forgiveness that you give that will you receive in return. Be mindful how you forgive one person and restore them full fold and forgive another and hold them at a distance; or as some would say 'draw a line of partition.' God is watching our every actions.

Take a breather, stop, and reflect on Luke 6:38. This passage is not a parable, neither is it talking about money; as some scholars say, but about your substances overall. With that said, do not forgive because you want to be forgiven by God but because you have already received your forgiveness and have enough to spare when forgiving others.

On that note, first write the percentage of forgiveness that you would like from God. Then list the names of at least three persons who have hurt you. If it makes you feel any better, write what they did to you. Finally, write a percentage out of one hundred that you have forgiven them.

What percentage of forgiveness do you want from God today?	Name of a person who hurt you	What did that person do to you?	What percentage of forgiveness did you give?

If you are not able to forgive men their trespasses, how do you expect God to forgive you your faults (Matthew 6:14)? People who are hurting hurt others, and it is not the will of God to see us hurting. If you nurture that hurt long enough, it will mature into a strong man, making it difficult for God to begin the healing process in your life. The sooner you seek help and let the hurt go, the quicker you start forgiving and loving again. God knows that it is unhealthy for us when we do not forgive.

Being a child of God does not change the fact that you are also a human being, and thus will hurt like anyone else. But if you are willing to allow God to work on your vessel, it will become easier to look your accuser in the eye and dress their wound. You might even become an advocate in helping others with their hurts. This will not only begin the healing process of forgiving others, but will also cause you to start loving yourself again.

You are now at the point of telling Daddy what's happening in your heart and that you are at His disposal. He can have full access to change what needs changing in your broken life. *"The Potter wants to put you back together again."* The Potter's House Tramaine Hawkins (Jeremiah 18: 1-6).

6. "And lead us not into temptation but deliver us from evil." Trust God to guide your footsteps away from temptations and to rescue you from evil. For God to successfully accomplish this action in you, you must give Him complete control of your everyday journey. Build a relationship with God by simply asking His approval on everything. People might call you fanatic, but that's okay. The Christians before you were called worse. It is okay to tell Him that you are going to the corner shop, or to ask Him what to wear to an occasion. An up-close and personal

relationship with Christ at this point is very critical. Your spiritual survival depends on it.

What sense does it make if your Lord says 'yes', but you say 'no'? If He says, 'don't go,' and you 'went'? What a tussle that relationship would be—repeated disobedience, and one failed test after another. God is too intelligent for that. He helps only to the extent you let Him. Remember that you can see to the end of the road, but God can see around the bend and, by extension, into your future.

"Let no one say when he is tempted, "I am being tempted by God" [for temptation does not originate from God, but from our own flaws]; for God cannot be tempted by [what is] evil, and He Himself tempts no one" (James1:13 AMP). Yield your understanding to His leading and instructions for the rest of your life.

7. "For thine is the kingdom, and the power, and the glory, forever. Amen." End your prayer by submissively giving thanks for time well spent with Abba Father. There should be no limits to your offering of praise to God. Praise is comely regardless of the circumstances (Psalm 33:1). We might battle in prayer about one thing for a long time (as we measure time) without results, yet we keep going back to Him about that same thing. Apply that habit to your worship and praise for God. Keep in mind that worship is a lifestyle, and your praise is an act of thanksgiving. Allow your worship to be seen by others daily and praise to flow freely from your heart. If you can differentiate the two, you will grow to appreciate

their functions throughout your life. Several battles could be won during your praise without one word of prayer being uttered (2 Chronicles 20 and Joshua 6:1–27). Praising God is not a matter of when you feel like it, but your given right to perform daily.

Do you want to do that which feels good or that which is right? Honestly answer the question. _____

___

At the end of all your prayers, remember to thank God, knowing that He has heard and will answer in due time.

The ACTS Prayer

Though the first printed copy of the ACTS prayer was believed to have been published in 1883, research of its author is still unknown. From the 19th century or beyond; the method is still effective today. Its technique is simple and easy to learn. ACTS is the acronym for adoration, confession, thanksgiving, and supplication. It somewhat patterns the method Jesus gave us in Matthew 6:9–13 by beginning with worship, openly revealing who we are, been grateful in all things and making your petition known.

1. *Adoration* reminds us to begin our prayer with high regard for Almighty God. Its wholeheartedly telling God who He is throughout the world and the universe at large. We exalt Him as Father and Lord over and of all (1 Chronicles 29:11–13).

2. *Confession* is honestly telling God your deeds. It shows your complete dependence on Him to survive your life's struggles. The apostle Paul cried out to God to be delivered from carnality (Romans 7:14–25). If we reflect, we will realize that the things that hurt us the most come from within. Notice the constant struggles we battle in the mind; it is a never-ending war, the spirit against the flesh and vice versa. Therefore, sometimes our prayers should be asking God to deliver us from ourselves.
3. *Thanksgiving* is the willingness to be grateful. Some people struggle to be appreciative. As a young believer in Christ, you have a lot to be thankful for. Reflect on the times you could end up in the hospital and didn't, you were at your wits end and you got that phone call, your child was sick, and you had no money, but the bills were paid. Needless I say anything else. To express gratitude from the heart glorifies God. In all things give thanks (1 Thessalonians 5: 18 and Psalm 92:1). You may say it is easier said than done but make it a part of your life and see overwhelming changes begin to take place.

Begin this seven-days challenge: each morning, write a list of seven different things that you can give God thanks for. Do not break the trend once you have started. Call up a family member, a childhood friend, or an old neighbor and ask them to remind you of some of your past blessings if that's what it takes to spark your memory. You might wow yourself or stand in awe.

In episode 9 of Teach Them Diligently the Transform Journal on Thanksgiving quoted, "This first mention of Thanksgiving in the Bible is when God instructs Moses on the Thanksgiving Offering. This is the beginning of our series on "gratitude"! So, join us for this foundational study on Thanksgiving for Families! (Leviticus 7: 12-15)

There are few things that will impact your life more positively than understanding and cultivating thanksgiving in your own heart and mind. The ripple effect of a thankful heart can be seen not only in you, but also in the lives of those around you. So, let's start today!"

4. *Supplication* is making petition to God for your needs and the needs of others (Psalms 142:1–2 and 30:8). I strongly believe that if I pray for others and do not have the time to pray for myself, God will raise up someone to pray on my behalf. Hence, do not get weary if you pray for others first and yourself last or not at all. God, who knows all things, will reward you accordingly. Do not be a bully, nor try to intimidate God (Deuteronomy 10:17). He knows your heart and its intent. Go to Him earnestly and in humility when making your request.

Please take a break and write at least seven words that you could use to adore your heavenly Father. Do your research and find other words of adoration that you could use. The sky is the limit. In the same breath, list some weaknesses in your life that are currently causing a distraction in your walk with God. Be specific. He would love to hear the truth from your mouth, confess it all. Letting the devil hear you telling God about your faults will allow him to realize that you are no longer willing to carry any secrets for him. You might completely be delivered from a sin or weakness that otherwise could land you in hell.

In addition, do not forget to be thankful for all His benefits toward you, your family, friends etc. Do not only thank Him for the so call 'big things' (1 Thessalonians 5:18 NLT) No! Thank God for the things that seem insignificant also. In other words, thank God for your thumb and the ability it gives you to grab hold of things. Consider nothing too small to thank Him for. Finally, write your supplication list. Ask your Abba Father. He is aware of your needs but would not mind you conversing with Him about those desires (Galatians 4:6–7). He is waiting to grant you them.

The Five-Finger Prayer

Pope Francis wrote the five-finger prayer for children, and it is effective for adults too. Though its instructions are simple, it hold power.

1. When you hold your hands up in surrender to God, you will realize that your thumbs are turn in toward you. Pause in that position and start praying for those closest to you. If at any time you think

you might forget those who are in your circle, note your family (immediate and extended), friends, schoolmates, coworkers, church family, neighbors, and so on. These people impact your life as much as you influence theirs. Now go ahead and pray for them.

2. Next in line is your *pointer* or *index finger*. Your pointer finger, as the name suggests, should point people in the right direction. However, in many situations that's not the case. It is our responsibility as Christians to pray for those who teach, instruct, and/or direct us. They include schoolteachers, pastors, parents, police officers, and such like. For example, our children are exposed every day to a playing field on which they cannot defend themselves. They are prey to a wide range of instructors, some with good intentions and some with ill. For that reason, pray for and against those who are daily pointing the children in a right/wrong direction. Do not wait for tragedy to present itself before you start praying for godly leaders to govern the world today and the generations to come.

3. The *middle finger* stands tallest and thus represents leaders: bosses, supervisors, ministers of the gospel, judges, lawmakers, presidents, prime ministers, parents, principals, just to name a few; and in this era, there are some leaders that defy God's righteousness. Notice that there in an overlapping of the individuals that you are praying for. Thus, there will be no escape of anyone when prayer is done. Let us stand together

in prayer, knowing that God is knowledgeable of everything, despite what is happening in this past, present, and future world. Being a babe in Christ, you are not asked to pray like the stalwarts. But be in agreement with them while they pray, clearly stating, "We are together in this until God's kingdom is come! AMEN."

4. You are now at the *ring finger*, which signifies several things, such as marriages, widowhood, children, the weak, and the sick. Get a small container with a handle and fill it with water. Now try to lift the container using one finger at a time. See which finger is the weakest at work; even the pinky will do a way better job than the ring finger. The ring finger represents individuals who are not able to stand on their own. You will see the need for prayer in the struggles that: marriages face, the loneliness of widows, pain during sickness, abuse of the weak and the cries that our children experiences.

5. Last does not necessarily mean least, because losing your *pinky* can be quite devastating. You have reached the finger that represents you. You are first and foremost the most important person in the world. You are the one offering up prayers on behalf of others. You are the one making a change in this world so that there can be a better tomorrow. I am aware that praying for yourself can be challenging; most people would rather to talk about others than themselves (Matthew 7: 1–5). You will not surprise God with what you have to say about yourself. He

already knows who you are. But for a healthy and a free-flowing relationship, keep telling Him about your ins and outs, ups and downs, goods and bads, wrongs and rights. It's a never-ending list. Now that you can talk with God for yourself, go right ahead and do so.

Who knows you, like you? Choose your posture, tone, and/or environment, and talk to Him. Be it soft or loud, long or short. Just talk to your heavenly Father. Do you know your God-given gift (s), and whose you are in Christ? What are your spiritual, physical, financial, physiological, and emotional needs? Are they all being met?

You will be surprised to know that God is interested in the simplest aspects of your life. You are at liberty to ask Him what to wear to a function, listen for an answer and obey His voice—you will never regret it. Pray for doors to be open or shut. Pray against all generational curses, and call what is not as though they are, in Jesus' name (Romans 4:17b). Amen!

PUSH

PUSH—Pray Until Something Happens—is considered an intercessory way of praying. Believers who PUSH are given the natural ability to continue one prayer for days, like Daniel (Daniel 10:1–21). Not knowing that his prayer had been answered the first day, he continued to pray for the next twenty days without stopping.

A woman in labor pushes to deliver her child whether she is told to do so or not. It is innate for us to travail in prayer when trouble comes. The tears roll naturally, nightly sleep disappears, and food no longer entices us. First Thessalonians 5:17 implores us to be in prayer during our daily routine. To be instant in prayer (Romans 12:12) does not mean that you are going to disturb others in your environment to show how godly you are, but rather that you remain prayerful in your heart and mind (Matthew 6:6). It was not a coincidence that in 1 Samuel 1:1–20, Hannah prayed in her heart. It was a weapon or strategy used to confuse and defeat the enemy, who larks around to hear our prayers. At times he declares war against our requests to God, like in the first chapter of Job.

Continue PUSHing like your existence depends on it. Lift your faith and believe Abba Father, and you will see enormous results.

Intentional Prayer

Intentional prayer implies to a request for prayer on a particular matter. Approach this type of prayer as a lion would approach its prey: focused, premeditated, and timely.

It is a challenge for some people to stay on track when they are asked to pray on a specific topic. We are sometimes carried away during prayer, but prayer should be treated with discipline and reverence, like any other ministry in the church. It should not be taken likely.

A few words of prayer in obedience to instructions are more effective than an hour of bobbling without any direction. If you are being led by the Holy Spirit (which you should be), follow where He leads and pray accordingly. Do not lose focus, God is not the author of confusion (1 Corinthians

14:33). He will put into your spirit the channel of prayer that you should pray.

For example, if you are asked to pray for the 'men,' you could be looking at grandfathers, fathers, sons, uncles, nephews, male children born and yet to be born, saved and unsaved, married and single, young and old, men in bonds and free, law makers and breakers, men you know, and those you don't, those in the security forces, health; It's a never-ending list. With the aid of the Holy Spirit, you will never run out of specific men to pray about; you're only constrained by time.

It is of vital importance that we do not step into another domain, since that appeal may be reserved for a different person to pray about. If at any time you are with a group of believers and you are asked to pray for someone, let one person pray while another watches and the third person confirm. It can be confusing for a sinner to remain focused when several people are praying at the same time. The sinner needs to hear the prayer being prayed over their lives and/or situation(s). That prayer in their hearing might bring about eternal change—even bring them to Christ Jesus.

Notes

Chapter 3
FASTING

Fasting is abstinence from food or drink for a period of time. Reasons to fast may vary among individuals for health, ritual, ethical, and religious purposes.

A fast must have a purpose before you begin, or it is merely a starvation. Why are you fasting? This self-denial practice may last for a few hours or for days, depending on its purpose.

A fast is a sacred moment between you and God; thus, it should not be shared with everyone. Matthew 6:16–18 describes a simple outline of what your countenance should look like during a fast.

Fasting is beneficial for both body and spirit once the right applications are implemented. If, as a new believer, you realize that your soul needs to be refreshed, revitalized, and rejuvenated by God, then deciding to go on a fast on your own displays' maturity. It takes self-denial and self-discipline to leave natural food for spiritual nourishment (Matthew 5: 6). Just remember that you can lose out on a spiritual outpouring if you do not fast, but there will always have natural food awaiting you after a fast.

It is advisable to forsake some things when you are on fasting.

- Stay away from distractions as best you can.
- Avoid social media such as Facebook, YouTube, and Instagram.
- Do not tell others, especially if they are not included in the fast.
- Refrain from walking around with a sad expression that express, 'I am hungry.'

- Do not store up food that you will eat after your fast. It will remain in your subconscious thoughts throughout the fast and defeats the purpose.

Can I Fast without Praying or Reading My Bible?

The answer to this question is both yes and no. Yes, because a person can fast medically without praying or reading their Bible and still get a good result if they follow the guidelines given to them by their doctor. People commonly fast before certain blood tests and surgical procedures.

On the other hand, since our focus is on fasting in the spiritual realm, the answer is no. An abiding Christian cannot fast without praying and reading their Bible.

Staying away from food means denying your body physical nutrition in order to feast on spiritual nourishment. What does your spiritual being need to grow? Your spiritual being needs to be obedient to the things of our Lord and Savior Jesus Christ, including reading the Word of God, praying, fasting, and being watchful. Without prayer and Bible reading during your fast, it will result in you starving the spiritual being within you, which will later suffocate Him in the long run (Joel 2:12-13). Remember that the kingdom of God is neither meat nor drink, but righteousness, peace, and joy in the Holy Spirit (Romans 14:17 KJV).

Why Do I Need to Fast?

The reason to fast is that it is an effective way to grow in God. Battles are fought and victories won during fasting and prayer. Jesus set a prime example of how to defeat the devil's schemes after His forty days and nights of fasting and prayer in the wilderness. (See Matthew 4; 17:15–21; Esther 4:13–17 and chapters 5–8.)

When and How Long Should I Fast?

There is no set day or length of time for one to fast. It is a personal choice. Notwithstanding, if you join a collective fast led by your local church, you will have to follow the time, day, agenda, and place (Acts 12:1–19), set by them.

A Few Types of Fast

Types of fast can vary across spiritual and health regimens. Spiritual fasts, for Christians, are based on biblical principles. Among the most common types of spiritual fast are partial, complete or absolute, and collaborative.

If a fast does not change your walk with God in a positive way, *STOP!* Seek advice from an elder or minister. Fasting leaves an opening, a lingering and longing void that seeks to be filled. If that emptiness is not filled with the things of God, the enemy will find place to play games and mess you up. Sooner than later, you will become a forever infant with no ability to grow in Christ when the devil comes in.

As a new believer in Christ, your spiritual growth may be

slow, but it should be a steady and gradual upward climb in God. Choose the type of fast that is best for you. You may make use of them all at various points in your life.

Partial Fasting

As the name suggest, a partial fast means excluding part of your usual food intake. A person on a partial fast may drink juice, eat fruit, or suck on a hard candy periodically. This kind of fast is normally practiced when one is on the job and in constant dialogue with others during the time of fast. It makes the stomach stronger and the mouth fresh. One needs to be careful with this type of fast because the quantity of intake may break the fast, making it null and void.

Another approach to the partial fast is choosing a fast of a specific length—for example, a twenty-one-day fast—and extending it. The individual may fast for three days, break for a day or two, and then continue the fast. Such a fast may yield health results, but I would argue that the spiritual benefits are questionable. Not that spiritual gains are impossible, especially if that is the only way you are able to access a fast based on health reasons. Do that which is necessary for you to grow in God. If you are taking prescribed medicines, please speak with your doctor about the best time periods that you could fast and if you are able to do so at all. Overnight could be your best yet.

Absolute or Complete Fasting

An absolute or complete fast involves consuming no food nor drink until the fast period is ended. If the fast begins at 6:00 a.m. and ends at 2:00 p.m., then the intake of any type of food will cease for those eight hours.

Note that eating just before you begin a fast can make you feel lethargic. You might end up sleeping instead of praying. Space your natural food and the spiritual feast. I suggest that you eat at least four to five hours before you begin your fast. You could also move out of an overnight sleep into your fast. If you are planning an evening fast starting at 6:00 p.m., eat your last meal at approximately 2:00 p.m.

It is advisable to limit a fast of this nature to no more than three days and/or nights maximum. In addition, you should remain indoors where it is cool, take a sip of water periodically, and refrain from overexertion or additional physical activity for the period of the fast. Just spend the time lying before the Lord in prayer and reading of the Word.

Collaborative Fast

A collaborative fast is undertaken by a group. The pastor or leader of the group will call the fast for a particular reason. It is imperative that the person in charge give a valid reason, time limit, and meeting point(s) before proceeding.

As a new convert, you should bring your participation in any collaborative fast to the knowledge of your leader if they are not the one who ordered the fasting. You cannot afford at this early stage of your walk with God to be in any kind of rebellious movement with any disobedient subgroup(s) in the church. Standing together can bring about lasting results, as in the book of Esther or on the day of Pentecost in Acts 2. Unity with the wrong crowd can cause destruction as in Exodus 32 and Genesis 11.

It helps a lot if you prepare your stomach for fasting. For example, you know you are going to be on fasting Wednesday morning, have soup, porridge, fruits and salads at least two days prior. It will send a single to your stomach that you are cutting down on the amount of food it will receive in short order.

Note, Do not store food to eat after fasting. If you fast through breakfast and lunch, your next meal is dinner, eat only dinner. This does not necessarily mean the type of meal 'big; three course meal,' but the time when the fast is broken. Do not preserve your breakfast and lunch, add dinner to them, and then eat all at the end of your fast. You will hurt your stomach. Rebuild the system by drinking and eating small (preferably) warm portions of soft meals. Married couples are required to seek each other's permission when going on fasting, and then coming together again (1 Corinthians 7:5).

Notes

Chapter 4
READING AND UNDERSTANDING THE WORD

We must first declare that Jesus is the Word, and the Word became flesh and dwelt among us (John 1:1–14). Therefore, if the Bible that contains the Word is treated as suggested, all honor will be given to God every time we open the Bible to read and understand the Word.

As a babe in Christ, it is imperative that you search the scriptures, for in the Word you have eternal life (John 5:39–47). It is of utmost importance that you explore the Bible for yourself, so you can ensure that whatever you are taught is the correct information. Before you get caught up in any heated biblical discussion, ask a few questions:

- Is this the Word of God?
- Does scripture say that?
- Can I find that verse if I search the Bible?

Note that in some cases, even Christians may quote words from a song and call them Bible verses.

Reading is not merely recalling words, but comprehending what the text is intended to convey. In the case of the Bible, you have a Helper, the Holy Spirit, who is willing to guide you if you allow Him to do so. The Holy Spirit teaches and reveals all truths found in scripture. Consulting multiple Bible translations, commentaries, concordances, guides, handbooks, dictionaries, atlases, and doctrinal books will enhance and expand your scope, but not like the Holy Spirit does. Only He can give a thousand revelations found in one scripture verse. Our brain's capacity is too limited to do such an amazing job, regardless of the books we read, compose, or study.

In fact, knowing what theologians' thoughts are regarding a particular scripture passage is good, but these are the opinions of other humans and not necessarily God's. Logos is a Greek word referring to the written component of God's Word (John 1:1-5), while Rhema is the spoken dialect (Luke 5:5) and the Paraclete 'The comforting Holy Spirit' (John 14:16, 26; 15:26; 16:7). God inspired men to *write* as He *speaks* whereas the Holy Spirt *teaches* (2 Timothy 3:16-17). Understanding the word of God is reveled in the changes seen in one's life transformation. I dare you! Intentionally start clothing yourself with the word of God as you read it daily, and the world will have to take a second look when they see you. The difference in you will glow, blossom and bloom as you pass by. The Word in you can never be hidden.

As a newborn babe, you may find reading and understanding the Bible difficult at first. But if you allow the Holy Spirit in, He will do phenomenal with your brain. As you become more mature in your walk with Him, He will divulge the wonders of His Word to you. Second Timothy 2:15 KJV declares; study to show thyself approved unto God.

Get familiar with the Word of God for yourself. This will allow you to better recognize when someone is quoting scripture inaccurately or falsely claiming 'The Bible says.' Asked your Bible study teacher to give you the reading prior to the next week's lesson so you can read ahead of time. This will allow you to better understand their line of conversation as they teach.

If you are challenged by reading, download an app on your smartphone and listen to scripture being read to you daily. If you do not have a smartphone, tune your radio to a gospel station that occasionally reads and explains the scripture.

The psalmist says, *"Thy word is a lamp unto my feet, and a light unto my path"* (Psalm 119:105 KJV). This indicates that we must turn on the light of God's Word in our hearts so that we will be able to see where we are going in this dark world. For that reason, the Word became flesh and dwelt among us (John 1:14). Jesus did not leave with the Word. He, being the Word, left us the Comforter, who is the Holy Spirit, to teach us all things and abide with us always (John 14:16 & 26).

It is impossible to know the mind of God and His laws without reading the Bible. Ask the Holy Spirit to lead you to the scripture passages that you should read today, this week, and next month. The Word will heal, change, build, or enhance your character. Read aloud what Hebrew 4:12 says about the Word of God.

As you daily read the words of God, put them on like a cloak. It makes no sense you only 'read' (calling words) but 'study' (get deeper into its meaning) the word of God. The Word is not just for knowing sake, equip to teach others, but never seen as relevant enough for your effectiveness. The more you study the Word of God you need to start mirroring its character so that you look like what you teach (intentionally or unintentionally). Meditate on these scriptures, Hebrew 4:12, Romans 12:1, and 2 Timothy 3:14-17.

Notes

Chapter 5
TITHES AND OFFERINGS

Tithes and offerings in the early church were any possessions that the saints had and willingly gave to the work of God. The same discipline should form our characters today. This can be a touchy topic for some people, but it should never be so for the people of the living God, because it is clearly laid out for us in Malachi 3:10.

Some Christians think that if they give their time and talents, they don't need to give their money. That is a deception from the devil. First and foremost, we should give our all to the service of God. It is then, with wisdom, that God, through the Holy Spirit, tells us what, when, and to whom we give our all, time, talent, money, skill, praise 'everything'. As you give to the Lord's work here on earth, watch Him give back to you in good measure—pressed down, shaken together, and running over (Luke 6:38 KJV).

Money is a broad topic in the Bible. Let us name a few of money's characteristics.

- *Giving*: Proverbs 13:22, Proverbs 3:9–10, Acts 20:35, Luke 6:38
- *Refraining*: 1 Timothy 6:10
- *Losing*: Haggai 1:6, Proverbs 13:11
- *Borrowing*: Proverbs 22:7
- *Working*: Proverbs 13:11
- *Investing*: Proverbs 31:16, Ecclesiastes 11:1
- *Enjoying*: Ecclesiastes 5:18–20, 1 Corinthian 9:7
- *Lending*: Proverbs 19:17
- *Tithing*: Malachi 3:8-11
- *Counting*: Luke 14:28-30

Challenge yourself to find other scripture passages for the money topics above.

If the character of the tither is wrong, then the gift given will be contaminated. Watch against giving, angrily, forcefully, and/or bitterly. A tithe or offering will not yield you any fruit if you give it grudgingly (2 Corinthians 9:7). You should give with thanksgiving from the heart and joy in the Holy Ghost (Luke 6:38). Giving tithes and offerings will benefit you more than others (Malachi 3:8–12), you are the only one that will experience the open windows of heaven with all its blessings been poured out. We do not *throw* but *bring* or *give* our tithes and offerings for the upward development of God's work here on earth.

Notes

Chapter 6
TESTIMONY

A testimony is a declaration of the facts about an event that has taken place in one's life which is worth sharing. It is sometimes misconstrued that a testimony is always joyous news. Some are deeply disturbing and painful, but the honesty in the story can bring healing to the teller and hearer alike.

One must sometimes find courage in order to share his/her experience(s). However, with the aid of the Holy Spirit, it can be done with confidence and conviction that will encourage others to come and share in God's mercy.

Note that lives can be transformed through a Christian's testimony. Thus, you should never declare a lie in the name of God to prop up your testimony. Remember, false witnesses were revolted against in the Bible. Lives can be lost at the mouth of false witnesses (Acts 5:1-10, Psalms 27:12 and 35:11).

No message is as powerful as your personal testimony. Our testimony incorporates the past with the present and captures the attention of an audiences. Real-life experiences are powerful weapons to begin with. First Corinthians 2:14 KJV, tells us that the natural man does not understand the things of the Spirit. A simple testimony will pull the attention of an ordinary person and allowing the Holy Spirit to impact their heart spiritually. A testimony can bring deliverance, healing, salvation, blessings, and comfort to the soul of others.

Commonly asked questions about testimonies are:

1. What should my testimony entails?' *The truth*, to begin with. We should always tell 'the truth, the whole truth, and nothing but the truth.' We are not repeating the oath originated in the traditional law

jurisdiction primitive England, but rather from the standpoint of Psalm 19:7b KJV.
2. Who is my target audience?' *Every living soul* is your target. With all the other vernaculars, add sign language to your vocabulary if that's what it takes to testify of God's goodness to everyone. There are no limits to who should hear that God is:

- Jehovah, the Covenant-Keeping, Forever-Existing One, the Lord (Deuteronomy 7:9)
- El Shaddai, God Almighty (Genesis 17:1)
- El Elyon, God Most High (Genesis 14–20)
- El Elohim, the Living God (Genesis 1)
- Jehovah Jireh, our Provider (Genesis 22:12–14)
- Jehovah Rapha, our Healer (Exodus 15:26)
- Jehovah Nissi—the Lord is our Banner, Shelter, Coverage, Hiding Place, and Battle-ax (Exodus 17:15)
- Jehovah Shalom, our Peace (Judges 6:24)
- Jehovah Tsidkenu, the God of my Righteousness (Jeremiah 23:6, 33:16)
- Jehovah Rohi, the Lord our Shepherd (Psalm 23:1)
- Jehovah M'kaddesh, the Lord Who Sanctifies (Leviticus 20:8)
- Jehovah Shammah, the Lord is there (Ezekiel 48:35)
- Jehovah Sabaoth, the Lord of hosts (1 Samuel 1:3)

The Unique and Moral Attributes of God

The unique and moral attributes of God cannot be contained in any book not even the Bible; without limit they exist before time was instigated, in time currently and when time is all terminated for man.

The unique attributes of God can only be found in Almighty God. None of His creation is able to possess any of these characteristics.

- *God Is Omnipotent.* Power was not given to God; God is all-powerful by Himself, full stop. He has ultimate authority over everything (Jeremiah 32:17; Genesis 1:3–31; Mark 4:39; Luke 1:37).
- *God Is Omniscient.* God has knowledge of all things. Nothing is hidden from His infinite knowledge (Psalms 139:1–6, 147:5).
- *God Is Omnipresent.* He inhabits everywhere at the same time (Psalm 139:7–12; Jeremiah 23:24).
- *God Is Transcendent.* God is in every way different, independent and beyond known and unknown creation (Exodus 3:4–6, 33:23; Isaiah 6:1–3, 40:12–26, 55:8–9; Job 38:4–30).
- *God Is Perfect and Holy.* He is altogether without impurities (Leviticus 11:44–45; Psalm 145:17; Matthew 5:48).
- *God Is Eternal.* God has no end. He is from before everlasting, and after everlasting He will still be God forevermore (Isaiah 57:15; Psalms 90:1–2, 102:12).

- *God Is Triune.* He is One who manifests Himself in Three (Deuteronomy 6:4; Isaiah 45:21; Ephesians 4:6; 1 Timothy 2:5; 1 John 5:7).
- *God Is Unchangeable.* There is no change or turning in God's character (Malachi 3:6; James 1:17; Numbers 23:19; Isaiah 41:4).

The moral attributes of God can be similar to some of man's qualities. However, humans exhibit these qualities sometimes and only to some people, things and/or situations. Therefore, there is no comparison whatsoever between the moral attributes of God and the attributes of man. They are frail in man but significant in God.

- *God Is Good.* God's creation was good from the beginning of time (Genesis 1:4, 10, 12, 18, 21, 25, 31; Psalm 106:1; Mark 10:18). *Man's goodness can be seasonal.*
- *God Is Love.* God's love goes throughout the world reaching all nations, tribes, tongues, class, race etc.; whether we love Him or not (1 John 4:8–10; John 3:16-18; Romans 5:8). *Man's love is conditional.*
- *God Is Merciful and Gracious.* God always looks beyond our faults and supply our needs (Psalm 103:8; Exodus 34:6; Joel 2:13) *regardless. Man's mercy and graciousness is extremely limited.*
- *God Is Compassionate.* God is touched with the very feelings of our infirmities (Hebrews 4:15; Psalm 78:38; Matthew 9:36). *Man's compassion is restricted only by what applies to them.*

- *God Is Patient and Long-Suffering.* If patience and long-suffering had not been exercised in the garden of Eden, there would be no human race today (Genesis 3:8–13; Numbers 14:18). *Man's patience runs out at about the third strike.*
- *God Is True.* Let God be true and every man a liar (Romans 3:4), because He has established His word above His very name (Psalm 138:2, John 14:6, 17; Psalm 31:5). *Man's truth quickly changes when they are in trouble.*
- *God Is Faithful.* God assures His faithfulness toward humanity. In many cases we are the ones who fail to accept what He has given to us (Deuteronomy 7:9; Lamentations 3:23; Hebrews 10:23). *The faithfulness of man comes down to what they can get in return.*
- *God Is Just.* Only a just God can give just rewards to humanity (Deuteronomy 10:17, 32:4; Hebrews 6:10; Psalm 89:14; Proverbs 16:11). *Man's justice is proportional.*

No human always possesses any of these attributes. Only God Himself can do so.

3. 'When do I testify?' *Every chance you get.* Begin a simple conversation with a stranger. Tell them how awesome God is in your life for two minutes. You interact with hundreds of people throughout the day; target at least three of them and engage them in a friendly conversation about God's goodness. This will not only give you a chance to share God with

someone; but it will also build your confidence in accomplishing the Great Commission that Jesus left for us (Matthew 28:19).

Our testimony should vary in different settings. For instance, if you are at a fasting service, your testimony should take the form of a confession of weakness or struggle that you might need the church to help you pray through. On the other hand, if you are at a crusade, you may need to channel your testimony toward the goodness of God and how He is able to keep and care for His own. This kind of a testimony will encourage the unsaved and/or backsliders to come to the Lord.

Testifying of God's goodness can feel awkward at times because persons may say you are 'showing off.' Look at what the Word of God says about it in Psalm 19:7. The Holy Spirit will inspire you to share the most accurate testimony at the right time. Therefore, your testimony will accomplish that which it is sent forth to do.

Notes

Chapter 7
SANCTIFICATION

Do not beat up on yourself. Sanctification is a timely process. You will not be immaculate, completely changed, and fully delivered in a day, a week, a month, or even a year. Your building needs time to carefully, strategically, and skillfully designed, so that you can develop into that perfect and spotless being that God desires.

Note that it was possible for God to make heaven, earth, everything therein, *and* man in a minute or less. But He set an example for us to follow by doing it step by step, one day at a time. Then He stopped to reminisce, smile, and call it good (Genesis 1 and 2). He is willing today to complete the masterpiece He started in you before birth. It takes time to attain greatness. Just let go and let God have His way in your life (Jeremiah 18:1–6).

Do not misconstrued that 'taking your time' means been slothful or relaxed. Sanctification calls for assertiveness and determination in getting to that place where God wants you to be. *Set apart, holy living, called out, being like Christ*, an *exemplary* life are just few of the words used to describe what a believer should set out to become (1 Peter 2:9–12).

Ask God to wash you daily (Psalm 51). Name your sins, ask Him to forgive you; then readily accept that forgiveness. *If we confess our sins, He is faithful and just to forgive us our sins, and to cleanse us from all unrighteousness. (1 John 1:9 KJV).* We sometimes linger so long in a place of not forgiving ourselves that our lives look like those of the Israelites in the wilderness—they wandered for forty years with their blessing right next door (Joshua 5:6).

To reach sanctification, though, you need to avoid repeating the sin for which you have been forgiven. In doing so, you will soon realize that there are some sins that you will never commit now that you have yielded to a sanctified life in God.

Bad habits and sinful natures can be enticing, captivating and longed for. Therefore, they are hard to stay away from. Getting rid of them may require you seeking the necessary help needed to overcome its challenges. However, determination on your part to let go and stay true to the change; will get you to that place where you need to be. Sometimes it is difficult to break some internal struggles on your own, thus, seek and get the help you need to be delivered from them. Each shedding may take a different direction, cause a unique pain, or build a new character, but don't worry; just give yourself time to heal as you go along. Time truly heals.

Notes

Chapter 8
THE HOLY SPIRIT

The Holy Spirit should always be referred to as He or Him and never as an it. He is a part of the Trinity, holding the same reverence as God the Father and Son Jesus Christ.

You have to feed your natural body to remain alive. So it is with the Holy Spirit: you have to feed Him to prevent Him from dying in you. The Holy Spirit can only be fed with sanctified living, obedience to Almighty God, reading of the Word, fasting, and praying. The Holy Spirit is subjected to been aborted, assaulted, abused and/or raped if we keep sinning in and against the body (1 Corinthians 6:18).

The office of the Holy Spirit, as pointed out in John 14:26, is that He is a comforter who will teach us all things and bring all things to our remembrance. The more we rebel against the leading of Holy Spirit, the farther away from us He goes. He is an intelligent gentleman who will not force us to do anything against our will.

Indwelling and Infilling of the Holy Spirit

The *indwelling* of the Holy Spirit is the righteousness of God living within us, whether we acknowledge Him or not. Ponder these verses in your heart today: 1 Corinthians 3:16; 6:19, 2 Corinthians 6:16, and Romans 8:11. His intelligence allows you freedom of choice, so He will rest until you are ready to give Him the time of day. On a regular basis, He will attempt to get your attention, if He is unsuccessful, He will continue waiting patiently.

The gentle knock you felt on your heart door that drew you to accepting Christ as Lord and Savior is the indwelling of the Holy Spirit in action. That comforting love you felt when you were alone is the indwelling of the Holy Spirit drawing alongside you. Perhaps you are planning to do something wrong, and a voice says, "No, do not do that!" That's the indwelling of the Holy Spirit speaking to you. The stillness of peace and joy amid sorrow is the indwelling of the Holy Spirit offering comfort to your troubled heart.

On the other hand, the infilling of the Holy Spirit is a gift from God. Jesus promised to leave with us another Comforter when He departed earth. Acts 2 records His first appearance, which took place in the upper room at Jerusalem. Jesus prepared His disciples for the infilling of the Holy Spirit in Luke 24:49 and Acts 1:8.

The same gift-giving of the Holy Spirit is still in effect today. Being filled with the Holy Spirit will allow you to speak in a language different from your native tongue. This spiritual and supernatural power can only be interpreted by man sometimes, but always known by God Himself. For that reason, one can speak a language unknown to others or himself.

Known and Unknown Tongue

Known tongue is a language spoken which is identifiable by humanity. One can interpret this sort of linguistics, as specified in Acts 2:1-18. The festive season had drawn persons from different nationality and language to Jerusalem. Man to man they were able to hear their own language and could identify what the disciples were clearly saying. One man, 'Peter' was able to clear the air for them all; thus, speaking in all the other languages as the Holy Spirit gave him utterance. Each were then able to hear the good news of God, understanding what is required to serve Him, and in that day approximately three thousand souls were added to the church (Acts 2:41).

On the contrary, the unknown tongue is understood only by God. In some cases, not even the speaker knows the language, in other circumstances they are able to relate and/or interpret the conversation in that moment, but afterward forgets everything. Men standing around whether of high or low estate will not be able to interpret this communication with God and that individual (1 Corinthians 14:2 & 4).

This gift is given by God and should not be envied by another. There are indeed varying gifts, but one Giver, which is the Holy Spirit (1 Corinthians 12:4).

The infilling of the Holy Spirit is needed for effective church ministry and holy living. The freely given gifts of the Holy Spirit should not be used as weapons against another believer or their ministry. They should not be shown off to flaunt how spiritually empowered you are. Never be call a spiritual bully or a spiritual abuser in the house of God. Our gifts are given to enhance God's work here on earth, and not to make fellow believers feel like they are not worthy of the kingdom.

It is possible for someone to speak once in tongues, as the Holy Spirit gives utterance and seldomly speaks again in that fashion. It could be that that person is endowed with power from on high for their ministry (1 Peter 4:10). Speaking once, for ministry's sake, will give you the wisdom to spiritually accomplish that which God has entrusted to your office.

For example, Let's look at someone who is hospitable in

nature; that person will do exploits for God if they are filled with the Holy Spirit (Daniel 11:32). The service they offer will be far better and more effective than that of a natural person who is not spiritually able to discern (1 Corinthians 2:14). This is completely different from having the gift of speaking with other tongue.

The gift of speaking in tongues allows the gifted individual to speak on a regular basis, whether with the same tongue or in different languages. According to 1 Corinthians 14:1–40, we should desire spiritual gifts—all but tongues, because of the confusion that man will make it out to be. There is no confusion in the Holy Spirit, but man's limited capability to comprehend will cause them to misunderstand His leadings. Note that it was important for Peter to know several languages. He discerned through the Holy Spirit what the people around him were saying on the day of Pentecost; thus, enabling him to address his audience in their varying vernaculars (Acts 2:14–41). Peter's educational background did not enable him to articulate, but the empowerment of the Holy Spirit who sat upon him. If there are no interpreters; do not speak, Paul encourages. Tongues will cease, but love will not (1 Corinthians 13:8).

Notes

Chapter 9
COMMUNION

Communion is Christian worship in which bread and wine are consecrated and shared in memory of Christ's sacrifice on the cross at Calvary. It is a sacred, continued reminder that He made the ultimate sacrifice and will be coming back again. This form of Christian fellowship binds the church to the body of Christ through His death burial and resurrection. Communion should never be taken, but rather ***given*** or ***served*** (Matthew 26:26–28; Mark 14:22–24; Luke 22:19–20; 1 Corinthians 11:23–30). The Last Supper, the Festival of Unleavened Bread, or the Passover meal was the first established Communion, set by Jesus Christ Himself. The example is clear: a suitable place, the correct meal must be prepared and a worthy person serving it to others who are partaking of it with understanding.

Not everyone can make ready a Communion meal or prepare the place for this ceremony. The one who prepares Communion should be sanctified and know the sacredness of its ceremony. Nevertheless, an individual prayer of consecration is still their responsibility, before drawing to the Lord's table. As outlined in 1 Corinthians 11:34, take the time to talk to God before indulging in such sacredness. Eat not to your condemnation but to your healing.

Communion should only be shared amongst Christians. If a person has not been taught to understand John 6:51–58, he or she should not sit at the Lord's table. It is common among church leaders today to have everyone sit at the Lord's table without taking a few minutes to teach its importance before sharing the emblem of Jesus's shed blood and broken body. If those who serve Communion seek to be blameless and not to be held accountable for leading others astray, then they should enlighten those who approach the Lord's table and allow them to decide for themselves if they wish to leave or stay on those terms. Though Judas sat with Jesus and the eleven at the first Communion, it is not an example for everyone. Notice that after Jesus spoke, Judas remain and shared in the Communion, which later caused his demise (1 Corinthians 11:29).

Holy Communion must be treated with all reverence for the sacrificed Lamb of God. Read 1 Corinthians 11:17–34 slowly, verse by verse, with all righteous understanding.

No requirement should be placed on how often Communion is shared. It should be shared as often as your local church community desires.

Sharing into the death, burial, and resurrection of the Lord Jesus Christ could bring you complete deliverance, healing, and life. It could also cause your spiritual and natural death.

Which would you choose, life or death? Give an answer from your gut feeling: _____.

Be honest with yourself and do the right thing; you will later be respected for it. Take some time to fix the things that need straightening out. You owe it to yourself and others.

Notes

Chapter 10
DOCTRINE AND CHURCH CULTURE

A church's doctrine and its culture are the teachings of that religious group and how those teachings are expected to be accepted and valued by the body of people who worships there. Seek out how you can get a doctrine book from your local church, because one size does not fit all. Every religious group should have its own book of values, morals, beliefs, laws, and standards.

The importance of knowing your church's doctrine and culture is to prevent you from rebelling and openly disobeying the rules that govern where you worship (Numbers 16: 41-50). If the church's doctrine and culture do not line up with the Bible, think twice (2 Timothy 3:14–17). The Word of God should be every believer's guide through life. If your church's laws are not governed by Biblical truths, then that body of people might not stand the test of time. This lack of the Word can also cause you, as an individual, to lose battles and blessings (Hosea 4:6).

Do not settle in a church just because it makes you feel good. Salvation has nothing to do with feeling but faith. Seek a fellowship that will pull you up spiritually and set you on the right path with God (1 Samuel 2:22–25). It's better to be corrected (Hebrews 12:6) than to be cast into hell (Luke 16:23–26). You need to grow as a healthy spiritual being, not as a sounding brass and tinkling cymbal (1 Corinthians 13:1). Churches today make it their point of duty to preach what the people want to hear in order to keep a large congregation; but as a newborn babe seek to know more about the truth of God rather than 'feel good messages.' Bear in mind, that where you worship can shape you one way or the other, ask the Holy Spirit for guidance as to where you should settle for fellowship. It has been said that 'you can grow where you are planted.' Take it from me 'you can also die where you are planted' if you are not planted on the right soil. Where should a cactus be planted, a seaweed grows, a fish survives, or an ostrich lay her egg? You are a peculiar being who needs a special place and condition under which to appropriately manifest. I have no doubt that the sower in Luke 8:5-15 had good seeds to sow. However, the ground on which they fell were what broke some and build others.

Notes

Chapter 11
DISCIPLESHIP

While talent is limited for some, it is endless for others (Matthew 25:14–30). Do not covet your brother's ability. Use the little you have for the betterment of the body of Christ (Mark 12:38–44 and Ephesians 4:11–13). Seek to be empowered, anointed, and then appointed not long after you have accepted the Lord as Savior, so that you do not become an idler in the house of God (Acts 1:5 and John 15:16). Finding nothing to do in the house of God can make you the devil's play mate. He is going to mess you up, and then laugh at your stagnancy. At this point in your Christian walk, you are no more a babe but a mature servant of the Highest God, dedicated to work in the vineyard. Your days of drinking milk is coming to its end (1 Corinthians 3:2). This is your opportunity to grow in your salvation (1 Peter 2:2) and help to carry the responsibilities of a ministry or two in your local church. The fields are white and ready to harvest (John 4:35).

Ministry comes with responsibility, that only mature Christians can handle. Dedication, discipline and commitment are needed to drive you in fulfilling your God-given talents and skills (Hebrew 5:12). Whatever ministry you go into, you need the Holy Spirit to teach you all things and bring all thing to your remembrance in order to effectively function. He will guide you into all truth and enable you to righteously succeed in what you are called to do. The discipline to pray, fast, read your Bible, and exercise your God-given talent needs the Holy Spirit to help you through.

Though I agree with Brian Byersdorf when he quoted that,

> *"Church leaders and attendees alike have noticed that worship attendance has changed with the COVID-19 pandemic, with 21% of churchgoers still substituting virtual attendance for in-person attendance."*

The reality is visible, the truth is clear; I however, advised that you take all opportunities possible to go into the house of the Lord to fellowship one with another; *not disobeying the laws that governs the land* (Hebrew 10:25). It amazes me how persons can go to work, back to school, the grocery story, in store shopping, games, theater, gym, 'you name it,' and yet not able to return to the house of worship. Ask them why? 'I am protecting myself from Covid 19' they would answer. The devil is a liar. Continue to develop your skill given to you by God then seek every way possible to execute same to the Glory of Him. Salvation calls you to serve not be served (Mark 10:45). Whatever God has placed in you, give it to the service of the Lord.

Now that you are moving away from milk to solid food, show interest in the ministry that you would like to serve into. Let your passion takes you to that place of destiny; serve with all your heart.

Notes

AMEN

Answer Page

Chapter 1

- Is it necessary? No
- Will it bring glory to God? No
- Will it allow you to grow spiritually in your new faith? No

Chapter 2

To whom do you pray? The Almighty God

Make a list of the words, attributes, and names that you use to honor the Father of all fathers:

Examples could include Abba Father, King of kings, Lord of lords, Great God, Mighty Deliverer, Strong Tower, Savior, Master, Friend, Everlasting One, etc.

Table of Needs and Wants

For example: I **need** to be able to retain Bible verses for later use. I want new clothes to wear to church.

Table of Forgiveness

What percentage of forgiveness do you want from God today?	Name of a person who hurt you	What did that person do to you?	What percentage of forgiveness would you give to that person?
100%	Mr. John Smith	Told a lie on me	10%

Acknowledgments

First and foremost, I want to give all glory to the God of my salvation—the Lord Jesus Christ, who has made the difference in my life. He started a good work in me and will bring it to completion. I began learning to read and understand scriptures in my late teens and fell in love with the Lord all over again. The Holy Spirit became my best friend and teacher. I was in school and didn't knew it, I am so glad He never gave up on me. I am determined to go where God is taking me. Thanks Abba Father.

Thanks to my two children, Shantal and Romario, who with or without knowing helped me on this journey. *Children are an heritage of the Lord,…blessed is the man who have his quiver full on them (Psalm 127:3-5)*

Thanks to Bishop Marcia Gale for seeing potential in me and entrusting in my care all necessary responsibilities that were in line with my overall development. This book is written in your honor, my pastor. After you gave me a class of new believers to teach for one year, I drafted some topics and made a syllabus to give structure to each night's lesson.

You gladly approved the topics, from which this handbook is written.

A big thanks to two faithful women, Mrs. P. Ashman and Mrs. J. May Campbell. Your support as my prayer and Bible study partners have held my hands up and prayed me through this journey. In some instance, I knew you had more faith in this dream coming to life than I did. I appreciate your patience with me. I am sure that there were times when you both felt like laying hands heavily on me without the leading of the Holy Spirit, but you travailed with me in prayer instead.

Thanks to WestBow Press for taking interest in my work and helping to give it the jump start needed to drive it forward.

References

Bennett, A. Lucy, and Richard Harmsworth. *Call Him by His Name,* Copyright by Charles M. Alexander, 1921 Tabernacle Publishing Co., pg. 421

Comparative Study Bible, Revised Edition copyright 1999 by Zondervan.

Stamps, C. Donald. Wesley J. Adams, Stanley M. Horton et al. *The Full Life Study Bible*, King James Version. Copyright 1992 by Life Publishers International.

Stanley, F. Charles. *How to let God Solve Your Problems* by Great Commission Media 2008.

Francis, Pope. *The Five Finger Prayer.* URL, https://www.google.com/search?q=pope+francis+five+finger+prayer&tbm=isch&ved=2ahUKEwjov8-i9ZLvAhURN98KHQIPAn8Q2-cCegQIABAA&oq=pope+fr&gs_lcp=CgNpbWcQARgAMgQIABBDMgUIABCxAzIECAAQQzIECAAQQzIECAAQQzIICAAQsQMQgwEyAggAMgUIABCxAzIECAAQQzICCAA6BwgAELEDEENQ7f8QWIfZIm-

DoqiNoAHAAeASAAYIBiAGIHJIBBDM3Lji-YAQCgAQGqAQtnd3Mtd216LWltZ7ABALg-BA8ABAQ&sclient=img&ei=4N4-YOjPGZHu_AaC noj4Bw&rlz=1C1LOQA_enJM743JM743

Copyright 2021 Catholic Online. All materials contained on this site, whether written, audible or visual are the exclusive property of Catholic Online and are protected under U.S. and International copyright laws, © Copyright 2021 Catholic Online. Any unauthorized use, without prior written consent of Catholic Online is strictly forbidden and prohibited. *Permission granted*

Based on several research done, the origin of the ACTS prayer model is unknown https://www.google.com/search?q=+the+acts+prayer&tbm=isch&ved=2ahUKEw i3y4ja-JLvAhVGulkKHZoGBzcQ2-cCegQIABAA&o-q=+the+acts+prayer&gs_lcp=CgNpbWcQAzIE-CAAQQzICCAAyBggAEAgQHjIGCAAQCBAe-MgYIABAIEB46BggAEAcQHlCNlQJY0aMCY-MayA2gAcAB4AIABiQGIAaMFkgEDOC4x-mAEAoAEBqgELZ3dzLXdpei1pbWe4AQPAAQE&s-client=img&ei=euI-YLcmxvTmApqNnLgD&rlz=-1C1LOQA_enJM743JM74

Teach Them Diligently, developed by Harnessing Strengths 2021 pdf. Ep. 9 URL: teachthemdiligently.net

BibleRef, An Online Bible Commentary that You can Understand,_© Copyright 2002-2022 Got Questions Ministries. All rights reserved. URL https://www.bibleRef.com

Matthesius, Jurgen. *Push: Pray Until Something Happens.* Paperback pg. 256 Thomas Nelson 2014. URL: https://www.christianbook.com/push-pray-until-something-happens/jurgen-matthesius/9781400206513/pd/206510

The New American Bible: Washington, DC: United States Conference of Catholic Bishops, 2002. (7th ed.) Holy Bible: New Living Translation.

Byersdorf, Brian. *Church Executive Magazine.* Helping Leaders Become Better Stewards. April 14, 2022. URL churchexecutive.com

2021 *Church Executive Magazine.* All Rights Reserved. Content on this Website is copyrighted and may not be reproduced in whole or in part without the express written consent of the publisher.

Hawkins, Tramaine. Varn McKay: *The Potter wants to put You Back Together Again* The Potters House lyrics, capital CMG Publishing.

© 2022 Lyrics On Demand All lyrics are property and copyright of their respective authors, artists and labels. All lyrics provided for educational purposes only. Please support the artists by purchasing related recordings and merchandise.

source from URL: https://www.lyricsondemand.com/results.html?cx=partner-pub-1187925111528992%3A9654624337&cof=FORID%3A10&ie=UTF-8&q=the+potter+wants+to+put+you+back+together+again&sa.x=0&sa.y=0